20th Century
PERSPECTIVES

The McCarthy Hearings

Philip Brooks

Heinemann Library
Chicago, Illinois

Designed by Herman Adler Design
Printed and bound in the United States of America

11 10 09
10 9 8 7 6 5 4 3 2

Library of Congress Cataloging-in-Publication Data
Brooks, Philip, 1963-
    The McCarthy hearings / Philip Brooks.
        p. cm. — (20th-century perspectives)
Summary: Describes how Joseph McCarthy and his associates tarnished
reputations and ruined lives as they investigated potential communists
and Soviet spies in the 1950s, how the "witch-hunt" ended, and
its consequences.
Includes bibliographical references and index.
    ISBN 1-4034-3808-0 (lib. bdg.) — ISBN 1-4034-4178-2 (pbk.)
    1. Anti-communist movements—United States—History—Juvenile
literature. 2. McCarthy, Joseph, 1908-1957—Juvenile literature. 3.
Legislators—United States—Biography—Juvenile literature. 4. Internal
security—United States—History—20th century—Juvenile literature. 5.
Subversive activities—United States—History—20th century—Juvenile
literature. [1. Anti-communist movements—History. 2. McCarthy,
Joseph, 1908-1957. 3. Legislators. 4. United States—Politics and
government—1945-1953.] I. Title. II. Series.
    E743.5.B8 2003
    973.921'092—dc21
                                        2003009585

Acknowledgments
The author and publisher are grateful to the following for permission to reproduce copyright material:
pp. 4, 6, 8, 10, 11(both), 14, 15, 16, 19, 20, 22, 24, 27(t-r), 28, 29(both), 32, 33, 35, 37(both), 38,
39(both), 40, 42 Bettmann/Corbis; p. 5 Yevgeny Khaldei/Corbis; pp. 7, 31, 34 Hulton Deutsch
Collection/Corbis; p. 9 Catherine Karnow/Corbis; p. 12 The Herb Block Foundation; pp. 13, 30 Corbis;
p. 17 Hulton Archive by Getty Images; p. 18 AP/Wide World; p. 21 Joseph Sohm, ChromSohm, Inc/Corbis;
p. 23 Bancroft Library/University of California, Berkeley; p. 25 Swim Ink/Corbis; p. 26 AMR; p. 27(m-r)
Francis Miller/Time & Life Pictures/Getty Images; p. 36 LA Daily News/David Crane/Corbis Sygma; pp. 41,
43 Getty Images

Cover photo reproduced with permission of Bettman/Corbis

Every effort has been made to contact copyright holders of any material reproduced in this book.
Any omissions will be rectified in subsequent printings if notice is given to the publisher.

Contents

A Divided World

World War II allies

During World War II, hundreds of thousands of men from the United States, Great Britain, and the Union of Soviet Socialist Republics (USSR) fought side by side to defeat Nazi Germany. When Germany surrendered in 1945, soldiers from the U.S. and USSR shook hands and embraced, danced in the streets, and wept together for friends killed in action. Their leaders had worked together, too. President Franklin D. Roosevelt and then President Harry Truman; British Prime Minister Winston Churchill; and Joseph Stalin, ruler of the USSR, had united to save the world from the threat of fascism.

Winston Churchill, Franklin Roosevelt, and Joseph Stalin meet in 1945 near the end of World War II.

A new, cold war

But the United States and Great Britain soon ended their friendship with the USSR. From 1945 until 1989, the USSR and the United States prepared to fight one another in a possible World War III. Each feared that the other wanted to take over the world. They never actually fought with bullets and bombs. But their race to build more and more deadly weapons, and to influence events in other countries became known as the Cold War.

Two conflicting systems

The USSR operated under a communist system. The government owned most businesses, farms, and homes. Citizens were guaranteed a job, a place to live, and food. But Soviet citizens did not enjoy many of the individual rights guaranteed in the United States. Freedom of speech and religion, for instance, did not exist in the USSR. This clashed with the capitalist and democratic ideology of the United States. Under Stalin, communist rule was often rough, too. After his death in 1953, it was learned that he had killed millions of his own citizens.

Gradually, the world divided along communist and democratic lines. In countries where many people did not have enough to eat, where there was lawlessness, or where there was huge inequality, communism was an attractive possibility. Each side believed its system of government was the right one. Many Americans feared the USSR's goal was to spread communism throughout the world. Soviet leaders distrusted the United States, too.

The Rise of Joseph McCarthy

Joseph McCarthy was born in 1909 and grew up in the town of Grand Chute, Wisconsin. His family and most of those nearby were Irish farmers. He quit school at age fourteen to work on the family farm. Six years later, he returned to high school and managed to complete enough courses to graduate after just one year.

In 1930, McCarthy was admitted to Marquette University in Milwaukee, Wisconsin. He received his law degree in 1935. Just four years later, the one-time high school dropout won an election to the Wisconsin circuit court as a judge.

McCarthy served as a lieutenant in the Marine Corps during World War II. He would later claim to be a war hero—something the military denied. He returned to Wisconsin in 1944 and lost an election for the U.S. Senate. The defeat only made him more determined to be elected. Two years later, he was elected to the Unites States Senate.

A fast rise to the top

At the start of the Cold War, Joseph McCarthy was an unknown Republican politician from Wisconsin. But once he took up the fight against communism, he became famous. Five years after being elected to the Senate, he had made himself into one of the most powerful men in the United States. The young senator truly believed communism was a threat to American freedom and security. He also saw anti-communism as an opportunity to gain more power for himself and the Republican Party. He soon became well known among senators for his willingness to say anything to gain attention.

McCarthy warned that agents of the USSR were working in U.S. government offices, labor unions, the movie industry, and universities. According to McCarthy, these "disloyal" Americans threatened to weaken the foundation of U.S. democracy. "The communist party might well be compared to a huge iceberg in a shipping lane," claimed McCarthy in a 1947 radio address. "The most dangerous part of the iceberg is under the water and invisible..."

Secretary of State Dean Acheson became a favorite target of McCarthy. He was born into wealth and educated at Harvard University, with liberal beliefs. Acheson represented much of what McCarthy despised.

Proud of his humble beginnings, McCarthy disliked many members of the U.S. State Department, which handled foreign relations. He saw these diplomats as snobbish young men who had attended fancy colleges and looked down on "average Americans." A good deal of his early career as an anti-communist would be devoted to attacking such "eggheads," as he called them.

In many people's minds, McCarthy was a kind of policeman who protected "good" Americans from so-called "commies" and "reds" in U.S. society. Joseph McCarthy hated communism. Fighting against it would become his life's work.

After being elected senator in 1946, a happy McCarthy poses next to the kind of campaign poster that emphasized his wartime service.

McCarthy and the FBI

The Federal Bureau of Investigations (FBI) is the top law enforcement agency in the U.S. government. The man in charge of the FBI during the time of McCarthyism was J. Edgar Hoover. He agreed with McCarthy that communists in the United States were a threat to the nation's survival as a democracy.

Spies in the U.S.

J. Edgar Hoover, director of the FBI, was a strong anti-communist, and aided McCarthy during his hunt for communists.

During the 1950s through the 1970s, hundreds of Soviet spies did indeed operate within the United States. But secret agents from the U.S. Central Intelligence Agency (CIA) worked inside the USSR, too. McCarthy, Hoover, and others often greatly exaggerated the danger posed by these Soviet agents. They used the public's fear of communists to help their own careers. They promised to protect Americans in exchange for their votes or increased power to do what they pleased.

McCarthy got most of the publicity, but much of his power came from Hoover's access to FBI agents and secret files. Hoover's FBI agents supplied him with personal information about Americans suspected of being communists. Hoover then passed this information to McCarthy. Information about personal troubles might be used to humiliate a targeted person.

Watched by the FBI

Along with known members of the communist party, those who worked for social change were especially likely to be watched by the FBI. Members of the civil rights movement, union leaders, or intellectuals became the subject of secret investigations. They were spied on and files were kept on such individuals. The files were filled with documents discussing their activities, the identities of friends and associates, and their personal habits. Foreigners who had emigrated to the U.S. from Eastern Europe were also not likely to be trusted by Hoover, McCarthy, and others.

The J. Edgar Hoover FBI Building in Washington D.C. The FBI investigated not only known communists, but also other people or organizations working for social change.

The American Communist Party

Founded in 1919, the American Communist Party (ACP) was a legal organization. It operated as a political party similar to the Republican and Democratic parties. ACP members competed in elections, including those for the United States presidency. The vast majority of ACP members were loyal Americans. However, they believed some of the ideas of communist thinkers like Karl Marx and Vladimir Lenin would benefit the nation.

In fact, the communist party in the United States had enjoyed a long tradition of being part of debates about how to run the country. Communist party members had served in the government and many of their ideas remain part of the government today. The communist party was active in helping workers achieve justice through labor unions. American Communists fought for civil rights for African Americans. The ACP was also strongly opposed to fascism. They had spoken out against Adolph Hitler long before most political leaders had taken notice of the threat he represented.

President Franklin D. Roosevelt adopted some ideas favored by communists during the Great Depression. Government help for the poor and government-created jobs helped many Americans survive economic troubles. Thousands of Americans were either members of the ACP, or worked alongside members at one time or another. These associations would later be used against them by McCarthy's forces. It should be noted that a few American communists did hope to see the violent overthrow of capitalism. In addition, the party tended to keep secrets. This looked suspicious to anti-communists.

Anti-communists wanted the ACP destroyed. The trouble was that to ban a political party was unconstitutional. McCarthy, Hoover, lawmakers, and private citizens found ways around this restriction. They could not outlaw the party, but they established various laws and publicity campaigns that made being a member uncomfortable.

Leaders of the American Communist Party leaving federal court in 1948. They were charged with plotting to overthrow the government and each was forced to spend $5000 bail.

The Smith Act of 1940 had made it a criminal offense for anyone to argue in favor of, or make any sort of plans to, overthrow the United States government by force. Hoover's FBI would use this law to prosecute communist leaders. Former party members came forward as witnesses to testify that this was the goal of the American Communist Party. The Smith Act and other laws like it were used to imprison leaders of the ACP and effectively destroy it.

Many of the party's top officials were eventually arrested on charges of conspiring to overthrow the U.S. government. Eugene Dennis, the head of the ACP, and eleven other high-ranking party officials were tried in the Supreme Court. All twelve were found guilty of conspiring to "teach and advocate" the "violent overthrow of the American government." By imprisoning or deporting most of the ACP's leadership, the government was able to destroy the party without having to make it illegal.

Eugene Debs, leader of the American Communist Party, arriving at courthouse for sentencing on July 2, 1951.

A brave voice

Supreme Court Justice Harry Black voted against the decision to convict Eugene Dennis and the other party members. He wrote in 1951:

Public opinion being what it is, few will protest the convictions of these communist petitioners. There is hope, however, that in calmer times, when present pressures, passions and fears subside, this or some later court will restore the First Amendment liberties to the high preferred place where they belong in a free society.

McCarthyism: the "Witch Hunt" Begins

On the attack

McCarthy rarely hesitated to attack anyone he decided was a communist. As a senator, McCarthy and other members of Congress often called special hearings to study the communist threat. Witnesses were called to testify at the hearings. A committee of politicians and government lawyers would listen to the testimony.

Witnesses at these hearings sat behind a table with a microphone placed in front of them. A line of congressmen and lawyers stared down at them from across the room. Witnesses were asked questions about their political activities and beliefs. Then they were asked about the political activities and beliefs of their co-workers, friends, and relatives. Many witnesses refused to answer such questions. They felt the committee had no right to demand information about their political beliefs or activities, and especially not those of their friends or family. Often the committee forced a witness to choose: answer all questions or go to jail.

"McCarthyism" was a term invented by a political cartoonist named Herb Block. In this cartoon, the Republican Party, symbolized by the elephant, hesitates to completely adopt McCarthy's policies.

"You Mean I'm Supposed To Stand On That?"

---from Herblock: A Cartoonist's Life (Times Books, 1998)

Many times the committee's investigation of a witness meant members already knew the answers to the questions asked. Answers then became a kind of test. If a witness admitted and regretted prior connection to the communist party, he or she would be dealt with less harshly by the committee.

McCarthy worked hard to expose communists and get them fired from their jobs. Many of those people called to testify were members or former members of the ACP. The vast majority of these people were loyal Americans—they had done nothing wrong. A tiny minority within the ACP actually did wish to overthrow the government of the United States. But McCarthy carelessly harmed countless innocent citizens in his pursuit of these few enemies.

McCarthyism

McCarthy's willingness to attack the reputation of anyone whom he disliked threatened the very freedoms and constitutional values he claimed to uphold. That is why the term "McCarthyism" has come to mean more than "anti-communism." McCarthyism refers to the use of lies and rumors, along with government power, to intimidate and silence political enemies or anyone considered by those in power to be "subversive."

The black silence of fear

In January of 1952, U.S. Supreme Court Justice William O. Douglass wrote an essay on the state of freedom in the United States. Titled *The Black Silence of Fear*, the essay attacked McCarthyism:

There is an ominous trend in this nation. We are developing tolerance only for the orthodox point of view on world affairs, intolerance for new or different approaches...

... We have over the years swung from tolerance to intolerance and back again. There have been years of intolerance when the views of minorities have been suppressed. But there probably has not been a period of greater intolerance than we witness today.

Douglass ended the essay with the following words: *Our weakness grows when we become intolerant of opposing ideas, depart from our standards of civil liberties, and borrow the policeman's philosophy from the enemy [Stalin's USSR] we detest.*

"I Have in My Hand a List…"

On February 9, 1950, McCarthy delivered a famous speech in Wheeling, West Virginia. He claimed that a number of employees in the U.S. State Department were communists. The State Department is the branch of the government that decides many of the nation's policies when dealing with foreign countries. McCarthy claimed that the Secretary of State—head of the State Department—was not interested in doing anything about communists in his offices.

McCarthy provides "proof"

Claims that the State Department included communists among its diplomats and staff had been made by other politicians. The difference was that McCarthy held up a piece of paper and said he was prepared to name these subversives. "I have in my hand a list of 205 cases of individuals who appear to be either card-carrying members or certainly loyal to the Communist Party," he announced to reporters.

No one had ever "named names" of the communists supposedly hiding in the government. In the days that followed his speech, the number of names on the list changed. In a speech before Congress a few weeks later, his list contained 81 names. Little or no evidence was offered to back up his claims.

President Truman on the defensive

McCarthy's speech in Wheeling and other pronouncements put President Truman in a difficult position. Truman was a member of the Democratic Party and if McCarthy could make voters believe he was "soft on communists," a Republican might win

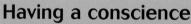

Having a conscience

Millard Tydings worried publicly that the few individuals McCarthy actually named would suffer unfairly because of McCarthy's careless charges. He believed the public needed to know that these people had done nothing wrong, but he feared the media would pay no attention. "The poor devils whose names were paraded across the headlines will be lucky if they get a mention on page 73 in the last column under weather reports," wrote Tydings.

the next election. Truman asked that a special subcommittee of the Senate's Foreign Relations committee investigate McCarthy's claims that communists were running the State Department and provide a report to the nation.

The committee was headed by a conservative and well-respected Democratic Senator from Maryland named Millard Tydings. It thoroughly studied the question for months. The Tydings Committee, as it came to be called, concluded that all of McCarthy's charges were "a hoax and a fraud." But by then, few people would listen to the truth. "The newspapers will not have time to print much of what I'm saying here today in rebuttal to five months of false smears and headlines," wrote Tydings in his final report.

McCarthy in a Senate sub-committee hearing where he claimed that another senator supported U.S. State Department communists.

Meanwhile, McCarthy made more wild charges. Again he had little evidence with which to back them up. He blamed the State Department and President Truman for allowing communists to take over in China. Many fellow Republicans, as well as Democrats, were becoming uncomfortable with his attacks. But most would not say so in the newspapers. When Millard Tydings suffered an election defeat due to his attacks on McCarthy, voices of disagreement among elected officials grew even quieter.

By 1952, even newly-elected Republican President Dwight Eisenhower preferred to avoid a fight with Joseph McCarthy. "I don't want to get in the gutter with him," he said. Many Republicans were happy that McCarthy's attacks had helped get Eisenhower elected, but they wanted now to stop hunting for communists in the government.

J. Edgar Hoover

No other American law enforcement official has ever had as much power as J. Edgar Hoover. Hoover was director of the FBI under eight different presidents, from Calvin Coolidge to Richard Nixon. Today the FBI headquarters in Washington, D.C., is named after him. He did much to turn the FBI into the best and most modern crime-fighting organization in the world. A strong anti-communist long before Joseph McCarthy, he greatly strengthened McCarthy and his allies during the 1940s and 1950s.

As director of the FBI, Hoover became one of the most powerful men in the United States. He often bent or broke the law to provide secret information about the activities of U.S. citizens to McCarthy and other anti-communists.

Hoover had nearly as much to do with the anti-communist fever that swept the country as Joseph McCarthy. Hoover's FBI provided anti-communists with private information on suspected reds. He often ignored laws protecting United States citizens from being spied on by the government.

Hoover was born in Washington, D.C., in 1895. He studied to be a lawyer. In 1917, he took a job with the Department of Justice. He worked as a special assistant to Attorney General A. Mitchell Palmer. In 1919, Hoover was put in charge of what came to be called the "Palmer Raids." The raids on homes and businesses led to the arrests of hundreds of foreigners suspected of being subversives. Hoover's days as an anti-communist fighter had begun.

The FBI

When Hoover took over what would become the FBI in 1924, he completely reorganized the agency. Along with improvements like a centralized fingerprint file, a crime laboratory, and a training school for police, he worked to make the FBI an important part of life in America. During the 1930s, he made himself famous by participating directly in the arrest of several major gangsters. He liked to pose for newspapers with a gun in his hands and soon became known as the toughest lawman in the nation.

His record as a "gang buster" made Americans believe him when he began warning that communism was the next great threat the country faced. Hoover gradually gained more and more power as he collected more and more embarrassing information about powerful people. Secret FBI files on the private lives of politicians made him a dangerous man to make angry.

After focusing on the fight against communists in the 1950s, much of Hoover's suspicions turned to civil rights leaders during the 1960s. He kept files on Martin Luther King Jr., Malcom X, and actors, singers, and writers thought to be subversives. Hoover died in 1972 while still in office as the FBI's director.

This picture shows the Boston Police in 1919. They are preparing to load "subversive" literature into a police ambulance. This shows that communism was thought of as a threat to the U.S. long before McCarthy appeared.

Hoover Testifies

In 1947, Hoover testified before the House Un-American Activities Committee (HUAC) about the dangers posed to the United States by subversives. In these portions of Hoover's HUAC testimony, one can see the way words were being used to stir up fear and patriotism among Americans.

The communist movement in the United States began to manifest itself in 1919. ... it stands for the destruction of American democracy;... it stands for the creation of a "Soviet of the United States..."

Victory will be assured once communists are identified and exposed,... Communism, in reality, is not a political party. It is a way of life—an evil and malignant way of life. It reveals a condition akin to disease that spreads like an epidemic and like an epidemic a quarantine is necessary to keep it from infecting the nation.

The House Un-American Activities Committee

In New York City, major Hollywood studio executives met and decided to take action against the Hollywood Ten rather than support their rights. They issued a statement announcing the firing of all ten and pledged not to hire communists. This was the beginning of what came to be known as "the blacklist."

United States lawmakers worried about the spread of communism long before McCarthy came to the Senate. As part of the effort to stop communist influence in the U.S., Congress created the House Un-American Activities Committee (HUAC) in 1938.

HUAC conducted searches for communists in the government or in labor unions, called witnesses to testify, and kept Americans reassured that the government was doing its best to find Soviet spies. The largely Republican committee used information provided by the Federal Bureau of Investigation (FBI) and the testimony of informants to find current and former members of the communist party.

In the fall of 1947, HUAC began looking into communist influence in the movies. Were communist writers and directors secretly filling movies with pro-communist messages meant to brainwash Americans? Movie stars, directors, and writers were called to testify. Ronald Reagan, Gary Cooper, and other stars pledged to do all they could to remove communists in the acting world. Studio executives, eager to avoid bad publicity of any kind, also pledged to help find reds in Hollywood.

HUAC and the Hollywood Ten

HUAC called a group of ten screenwriters, directors, and producers to Washington, D.C. for hearings The Hollywood Ten, as the newspapers called them, had all been members of the ACP. Alvah Bessie, Herbert Biberman, Lester Cole, Edward Dmytryk, Ring Lardner, Jr., John Howard Lawson, Albert Maltz, Sam Ornitz, Robert Adrian Scott, and Dalton Trumbo had scripted, produced, or directed hundreds of Hollywood films.

All claimed they had never attempted to brainwash anyone with their movies. They felt information about their political beliefs was none of HUAC's business. The First Amendment of the U.S. Constitution guaranteed the right to freedom of speech. The Ten thought the foundation of the U. S. involved protecting those taking unpopular stands or joining organizations that disagree with the majority.

The Hollywood Ten and their lawyers assumed the United States Supreme Court would uphold their right to freedom of speech and thus they refused to answer most of the committee's questions. During weeks of testimony, members of the Hollywood Ten and HUAC often shouted at one another. Several of the Ten believed the committee was acting in an un-American way.

The House of Representatives voted to cite the Hollywood Ten for contempt of Congress. They faced a trial and were found guilty in 1948. When the Supreme Court refused to review the ruling, each of the ten served a six-month prison term. After they were released, no studio in Hollywood dared to hire any of them again. From that moment on, HUAC had genuine power and struck fear in those called to testify.

Four of the Hollywood Ten on their way to jail to begin their jail sentences. Handcuffed in front are Albert Maltz and Ring Lardner Jr.

The blacklist

On December 3, 1947, movie studios that had employed the Hollywood Ten announced that all would be fired. These firings were the beginning of what would come to be called "the blacklist." Accused communists or former communists would not be hired to work in the entertainment industry ever again. The blacklist included the names of some of the most famous actors, writers, and directors in the United States. Here are just a few of the wide range of people who were blacklisted during the 1950s:

• **Alvah Bessie**, writer, one of the Hollywood Ten, and a member of the Communist Party.

• **Betsy Blair**, actor, never joined the Communist Party, but because of her leftist beliefs was blacklisted.

• **Marc Blitzstein**, musical composer believed to be a member of the ACP.

• **J. Edward Bromberg**, actor, never appeared in another film after being blacklisted, and died while appearing in a play by blacklisted writer Dalton Trumbo.

• **John Henry Faulk**, radio personality. He later sued CBS for firing him and won more than three million dollars. He spent years looking for work afterwards.

• **Dashiell Hammett**, author of detective books including *The Maltese Falcon*, was jailed for six months for refusing to testify. He never wrote again.

• **Rose Hobart**, actor, was blacklisted after communist documents which included her forged signature were filed with HUAC as evidence against her.

• **Dalton Trumbo**, writer, became the fist Hollywood Ten member removed from the blacklist. He later caused controversy when he said that everyone involved in the HUAC hearings were victims whether they were "friendly" or "unfriendly" witnesses.

The First and Fifth Amendments

During the late 1940s and early 1950s, a countless number of investigative committees were created by local, state, and federal government agencies in search of communists. Much of this had to do with politicians using their membership on such committees as proof to voters of their strong anti-communist feelings. Nevertheless, they had real power and ultimately threatened the constitutional rights of many Americans.

Taking the fifth

Before the Hollywood Ten were convicted and sent to prison, lawyers and witnesses had often argued that the First Amendment of the United States Constitution meant witnesses could not be forced to answer questions involving their political views, the organizations they chose to join, or the friends they chose to have. Witnesses who did not wish to answer HUAC's questions began announcing they would not answer, based upon rights granted to them under the Fifth Amendment. This was an important shift. The Fifth Amendment to the Constitution gives a witness the right to refuse to answer a question because to do so would reveal evidence against himself or herself.

This meant that witnesses "taking the fifth" gave the appearance that some sort of crime had been committed. To answer the question "Are you now or have you ever been a member of the communist party?" by stating that you planned to take the fifth amendment made witnesses appear to be hiding something. The question "Are you now or have you ever been a member of the communist party?" became a question that ruined reputations whether it was answered or not. McCarthy did his best to embarrass and bully such witnesses by loudly referring to them as "Fifth Amendment communists."

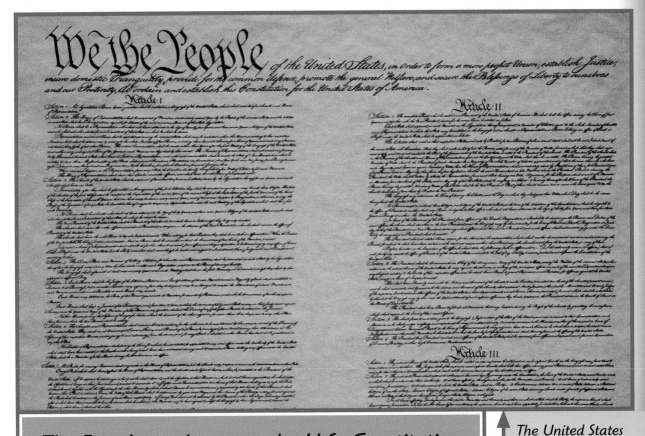

The First Amendment to the U.S. Constitution

Congress shall make no law respecting an establishment of religion, or prohibiting the free exercise thereof; or abridging the freedom of speech, or of the press; or the right of the people peaceably to assemble, and to petition the government for a redress of grievances.

The Fifth Amendment to the U.S. Constitution

No person shall be held to answer for a capital, or otherwise infamous crime, unless on a presentment or indictment of a grand jury, except in cases arising in the land or naval forces, or in the militia, when in actual service in time of war or public danger; nor shall any person be subject for the same offense to be twice put in jeopardy of life or limb; nor shall be compelled in any criminal case to be a witness against himself, nor be deprived of life, liberty, or property, without due process of law; nor shall private property be taken for public use, without just compensation.

The United States Constitution, which guarantees all basic civil rights to United States citizens.

Those who followed their consciences and refused to answer questions often lost their jobs and friends. Their spouses and children suffered, too. A college teacher later recalled how "old friends, fellow students, former colleagues, fled to the hills, in fact behaved like a bunch of frightened rabbits" after he took the Fifth Amendment while sitting before HUAC.

How Well Do I Know My Neighbor?

A series of laws were passed to prevent communists from gaining positions within the United States government or in schools and universities. Job applicants were asked to take oaths pledging loyalty to the United States. Some even had to take lie detector tests to insure they were not Soviet agents.

Loyalty and security

In 1947, President Harry Truman was under pressure to make sure that no communists were hiding in the government. Anti-communists claimed that the nation's Loyalty-Security Program needed to be strengthened. In response, Truman signed Executive Order 9835. The order increased the power of the FBI, which was in charge of enforcing the Loyalty-Security Program. The order stated that all government employees and those applying for government jobs would now be checked against the FBI's files. If any "derogatory information" was discovered, an investigation would start.

The order was written in such a way that nearly any activity the FBI found to be suspicious might lead to an investigation. As part of the increased security, the U.S. Attorney General was authorized to make a list of subversive groups. If there was evidence that an employee had associated with one or more of these groups, he or she was in trouble. Having been a labor union member, or having a friend or relative who had once belonged to the communist party became "reasonable grounds for belief in disloyalty."

Even the New York Metropolitan Opera Company thought it should watch out for communists. In this 1951 photo, chorus members take a loyalty oath.

Employees suspected of disloyalty were sent an official document stating the charges against them. An accused employee could request a hearing before a national Loyalty Review Board. Some employees who appeared before the board managed to keep their jobs. About 12,000 employees accused of disloyalty soon simply left their jobs rather than fight. Liberal groups fought against the practices, but more and more private companies adopted similar practices during the 1950s.

McCarthy in the classroom

In 1949, the National Education Association (NEA) and the American Association of School Administrators (AASA) sent a 54-page booklet to teachers setting guidelines for teaching "Americanism." The booklet stated that no school system should hire members or former

members of the communist party. At the same time, however, the NEA and AASA spoke out against groups or individuals claiming any teacher was a communist without real evidence.

In addition to these new instructions to teachers, HUAC demanded a list of all the textbooks being used in government, history, literature, social science, economics, and geography classes in 81 high schools. The books would be checked to see that they conformed to HUAC's vision of how an American child should be educated.

To avoid the possibility of being fired, many high school teachers made sure their lessons did not offer challenging questions about political ideas or the role of the United States in the world. Professors at colleges and universities were the subject of much more suspicion than high school teachers. Traditionally, college professors were thought of as liberals because many joined left-wing groups or even the American Communist Party (ACP).

The University of California at Berkeley decided that all professors should sign an oath of loyalty to the United States. Many professors rebelled. 26 Berkeley professors were "ejected" when they refused to sign. Another 37 soon resigned in protest. As a result, 55 courses could no longer be offered to students because the professors for those courses were gone.

Angry letters from professors across the country flooded the office of the University's president and advisors. Eighteen scholars signed a letter stating that they were "fighting for the principle that loyalty in America is to be judged by the substance of men's lives and actions." The university finally gave in. The loyalty oath was discontinued.

Professors and staff pack a 1949 meeting at the University of California, Berkeley, to protest the university's new policy that required loyalty oaths.

The Balance Tips

During the late 1940s and early 1950s, dramatic events made democracies throughout the world nervous. The USSR expanded its borders, taking control of Eastern Europe after World War II. China became a communist country in 1949. Communist North Korea attacked democratic South Korea. By the time the United States entered the Korean War in 1950, the world seemed on the edge of a third world war.

The Iron Curtain

The Iron Curtain became an actual concrete wall in 1962, when the USSR had the Berlin Wall erected to separate East Berlin and West Berlin. The wall came down in 1989.

During World War II, the USSR had been attacked by Germany along its western border. After the war, Soviet dictator Joseph Stalin feared another attack along its western border with Europe. To provide the USSR with more security, Stalin decided not to bring the Soviet army home. USSR tanks and soldiers remained in the countries they had liberated from the Nazis. Poland, Bulgaria, Romania, Yugoslavia, Czechoslovakia, and the eastern half of Germany became satellite states. The USSR made sure that communist governments ran these countries and used force when necessary to keep them in place. This created a safety zone between Moscow and the democracies of Europe.

The governments of Western Europe and the United States were angered by this abuse of Soviet military power. British Prime Minister Winston Churchill made a famous speech in which he claimed "an iron curtain has descended across the continent [Europe]."

Political posters like this one from China in 1960 made communist countries look aggressive and dangerous to Americans.

China goes red

Another blow to the confidence of the U.S. was the "loss" of China. In 1949, communist rebels led by Mao Tse-tung took over the country after a bitter civil war. The U.S. had supported Chiang Kai-shek, an anti-communist. Coming so near to the first Soviet nuclear test in the summer of 1949, the loss further shook America's confidence.

Many in the Republican Party argued that President Harry Truman, along with the State Department, had contributed to Chiang's defeat. Democrats, argued the Republicans, had failed to save China from the reds. In truth, Chiang's government had been dishonest and he did not have the support of most Chinese.

McCarthy was outraged at what he saw as intentional sabotage of the U.S. fight against communism. He again claimed that communists in the State Department sought to help communist leaders.

The Truman Doctrine

Communism was spreading. Most often, the threat came from inside a country and resulted in a civil war. In 1947, President Harry Truman pledged to help democratic forces facing communists. The USSR and China often helped communist armies with advice, weapons, and other supplies.

Communism, Truman claimed, was an evil system that led to low standards of living and a lack of freedom. The United States would stand up against it. The so-called Truman Doctrine meant that armies helped by the U.S. often fought directly with armies supported by the USSR or China. Civil wars in Greece and Turkey threatened to boil over into a larger war with the USSR.

The United States and China eventually fought directly during the Korean War. But it was not officially between those two countries because the U.S. fought as part of the United Nations forces. Fifty thousand American soldiers died in the war. More than one million civilians lost their lives.

This map shows the USSR's control of Eastern Europe after World War II. The line was called the Iron Curtain.

Key
— The Iron Curtain
→ Advance of the Red Army 1944–45
■ Communist countries
■ Communist but not under control of USSR
□ Capitalist democratic countries

NB: Austria was occupied by the U.S., USSR, Britain, and France until 1955 when it became independent.

NORWAY
SWEDEN
Moscow
North Sea
DENMARK
Baltic Sea
BRITAIN
NETH.
BELGIUM
LUX.
Stettin
Berlin
EAST GERMANY
POLAND
UNION OF SOVIET SOCIALIST REPUBLICS (USSR)
WEST GERMANY
CZECHOSLOVAKIA
FRANCE
SWITZERLAND
AUSTRIA
HUNGARY
Trieste
ROMANIA
YUGOSLAVIA
Black Sea
ITALY
BULGARIA
ALBANIA
GREECE
TURKEY

0 250 km
0 125 miles

Mediterranean Sea

More red panic

On May 19, 1950, in New Jersey, twelve train cars loaded with ammunition and explosives blew up while being loaded onto barges for shipment. Thirty people were killed by the explosion. Many residents of the town of South Amboy believed they were under Soviet attack. One man dragged himself out of the rubble of his house and found his wife standing on the front lawn screaming, *"The Russians are in town!"*

This photo shows UN tanks during the Korean War. The UN fought on the side of South Korea against North Korea.

Reds in Wisconsin!

In May 1950, the small Wisconsin town of Mosinee decided to launch an experiment. Residents wanted to warn the rest of the nation about the dangers posed by a communist takeover of the United States. So, the town "put itself behind an iron curtain for a day."

First thing in the morning, a group of American veterans used unloaded rifles and pistols to take over the town. They said they were claiming Mosinee for "The United Soviet States of America." For a day, they held the library, a mill, and local schools under "communist" control.

The local newspaper's name was changed for a day to the Red Star and was printed on pink paper. The town's movie theater was renamed The People's Theater and showed Soviet propaganda films. During the show, Stalin's face occasionally appeared on the screen. When it did, the audience was ordered to cheer.

A group calling itself the Security Police rounded up government, religious, and business leaders and kept them for the day in special concentration camps. A "Red" parade streamed through the middle of town and citizens were ordered around all day by "Red Police."

At the end of the day, the communist posters and barbed wire prison camps were torn down. Mosinee happily rejoined the United States. An article and photographs appeared in *LIFE* magazine about Mosinee's "red" day.

Nuclear Spies: The Threat Made Real

From 1945 through 1948, the United States was the only country in the world that had nuclear weapons. This huge advantage gave Americans a feeling of security. The USSR would not dare attack the U.S. when entire Soviet cities could be destroyed by a single bomb.

USSR goes nuclear

Then, on September 23, 1949, President Truman announced that the USSR had exploded its own atomic bomb. This caused a new wave of anxiety. America's feeling of security was now gone. School teachers in "target cities" like New York, Los Angeles, Chicago, Detroit, and Philadelphia conducted drills in the middle of a lesson. They would suddenly yell, "Duck and cover!" Students would duck under their desks and curl up. This was supposed to protect them from a nuclear explosion. Some families built bomb shelters in their backyards and stocked them with food and water to survive an attack.

Children in New York dive under their desks during an atomic bomb drill in 1951.

Many Americans and government officials refused to believe Soviet scientists had figured out how to build the bomb without help. Convinced that spies must have stolen the secret plans and given them to the Soviets, anti-communists began a hunt for spies.

A spy ring revealed

Investigations revealed Soviet agents had indeed attempted to learn the secrets of the bomb. In 1950 a British scientist named Klaus Fuchs was arrested. Fuchs had helped create the first atomic bomb the United States dropped on Japan in 1945. He soon confessed to passing secrets to the USSR. Fuchs's associate, a chemist named Harry Gold, also was arrested and confessed. Gold named David Greenglass, who had also worked at the Los Alamos Laboratories, as a co-conspirator. Greenglass soon confessed and claimed his sister's husband, Julius Rosenberg, was another member of the spy ring.

Based on Greenglass's claims, Julius and Ethel Rosenberg, the parents of two small children, were arrested for espionage. The two had been members of the American Communist Party (ACP). Had the two confessed, they would have served prison terms and eventually been released. But both insisted they were innocent. Americans were shocked when the two were found guilty of espionage and sentenced to death.

Klaus Fuchs was a British scientist who spied for the USSR.

It is reported that J. Edgar Hoover and lawyers for the prosecution had wanted to avoid executing the couple. Pleas came from around the nation to spare the Rosenbergs' lives, if only for the sake of their children. In the end, their lack of confession, along with the hysteria connected to the spy cases, led them to their deaths. The Rosenbergs were executed on June 19, 1953.

A scientist denied

Even Robert Oppenheimer, the famous physicist who had led the effort to create the first atomic bomb, came under suspicion. While a professor at the University of California at Berkeley, many of his friends and associates were or had been Communist Party members. The Atomic Energy Commission (AEC) investigated Oppenheimer. In 1954, the AEC refused to renew security permission that allowed him access to the government's scientific secrets. Oppenheimer was a prominent scientist in the United States, but was powerless against McCarthyist suspicion.

Korea Erupts

Douglas MacArthur with aides observing action against the enemy on September 14, 1950.

On June 25, 1950, war broke out in Korea. Communist troops from North Korea attacked democratic forces in South Korea. When North Korean communists threatened to overrun the country, U.S. troops entered the fighting as part of a United Nations (UN) force. UN soldiers fighting under U.S. General Douglas MacArthur made quick advances into the North. China grew nervous. Only the Yalu River separated North Korea from China. 250,000 Chinese soldiers crossed the Yalu River on October 16 and joined North Korean forces in pushing back the South Korean and UN advance.

The U.S. home front

In response to the start of the Korean War in 1950, several members of Congress proposed laws meant to make the country more secure. Many of the ideas from these proposals were put together into one package by Nevada's Republican Senator Patrick McCarran.

McCarran sought to stop communists from operating in the U.S. ever again by giving the FBI and other authorities more power. President Truman vetoed the McCarran Act. He was uncomfortable with the fact the bill gave the government new power to restrict civil liberties like freedom of speech. It even allowed the government to round up subversives and keep them in special concentration camps during a national emergency. Congress voted to override Truman's veto and the bill became law.

The war became a stalemate. McCarthy and Republicans blamed the loss of China to communism for causing the war in Korea. Communist North Korea, they argued, had been encouraged by Mao's takeover of China. McCarthy blamed Democrats and communists in the U.S. State Department for getting the United States stuck in the Korean War.

McCarthy on the attack

Once North Korean forces were pushed back behind their border with South Korea, President Truman wanted to end the fighting. General MacArthur, a war hero, publicly insisted this was a bad idea. MacArthur wanted to keep pushing ahead. He believed that North and South Korea could be reunited as a democratic state through a decisive military victory.

When Chinese troops entered the war on North Korea's side, MacArthur called on Harry Truman to order the bombing of targets inside China. He even said Truman ought to consider using nuclear weapons against China and North Korea. Fearing MacArthur's words might spark a world war, Truman publicly warned the general. MacArthur insisted the president was wrong. Truman fired him for insubordination. "You cannot appease or otherwise surrender to communism in Asia without undermining our efforts to halt its advance in Europe," insisted MacArthur in his farewell speech to Congress in April of 1951.

This picture from after the 1949 communist take-over in China shows Chinese people holding the Little Red Book, written by Mao Tse-tung to explain his ideas.

Joseph McCarthy was enraged by Truman's firing of an anti-communist hero. Following MacArthur's dismissal, McCarthy gave a blistering speech to the Senate. In the speech, McCarthy used the case of a specific U.S. soldier fighting in North Korea to emphasize his point that Truman's government was soft on communism. He blamed Secretary of State Dean Acheson for not allowing MacArthur to finish the job he began:

Today Bob Smith is at home in Middleburg, PA, but his hands and feet are still in the hills on this side of the Yalu [River]—a tribute to the traitorous red communist clique [group] in our State Department... I suggest that when the day comes that Bob Smith can walk, when he gets his artificial limbs, that he first walk over to the State Department and call upon the great Red Dean of fashion [Dean Acheson]... He should say, "Mr. Acheson, if you wish to perform one service for the American people you should not only resign from the State Department but you should remove yourself from this country and go to the nation for which you have been struggling and fighting for so long."

Alger Hiss vs. Whittaker Chambers

Alger Hiss was an expert on China and a United States State Department official. Hiss was also accused of spying for the USSR. Hiss's problems began in 1939. Whittaker Chambers, a former member of the American Communist Party, was called to testify before HUAC. Chambers, a senior editor at *TIME* magazine, confessed that he had spied for the USSR. He told the committee that Alger Hiss had given him secret State Department documents that he had later passed on to a Soviet agent.

The typewriter proves it

Hiss said Chambers was lying and took him to court for libel. During the trial, Chambers provided typewritten memos and summaries of State Department documents as evidence. Government experts examined Hiss's typewriter. They testified that Hiss had typed both the summaries and personal correspondence on the machine. Experts on Hiss's side argued that the typewriter had been altered to make it look like it was the machine used to produce the documents.

Alger Hiss (standing right) and Whittaker Chambers (standing left) confront each other at a HUAC committee hearing on August 25, 1948.

The pumpkin papers

By 1948, the Hiss-Chambers trials had led to a pumpkin patch on Chambers's farm in Maryland. There, hidden inside a hollowed-out pumpkin, was a container of microfilm. The film contained what would later become known as the "pumpkin papers." These were more State Department documents that Chambers claimed were given to him by Hiss.

Though he was never convicted of espionage, Hiss eventually served two years in prison for lying while under oath. He denied all charges against him for the duration of his life. Scholars and historians today continue to argue about whether Hiss was a spy. Soviet-era documents obtained from Russia in 1996 provided more fuel for the debate, but did not answer the question once and for all.

Richard Nixon, a senator from California, was assigned to HUAC. He became an outspoken anti-communist. Here, he examines microfilm found inside a pumpkin on Chambers' farm. Nixon became vice-president in 1952 and was elected president in 1968.

Owen Lattimore

Johns Hopkins professor Owen Lattimore was another of McCarthy's favorite targets. An expert on China, Lattimore had advised members of the State Department during Mao's takeover of that country. Though McCarthy tried for years to show Lattimore had betrayed the United States, no real evidence was ever produced. Still, Lattimore's career and reputation were damaged.

The Hollywood Blacklist

Four years after the Hollywood Ten were called to testify, McCarthy and HUAC attacked the movie industry again. He again claimed that Hollywood had many communists and that they were placing hidden pro-communist messages in their films. Negative images of the United States, McCarthy complained, had been purposely placed in films that would be seen in other countries.

HUAC had trouble providing specific examples of dialog or images which were pro-communist. Some HUAC members complained, for example, about a shot of smiling children in a film called *Song of Russia,* even though when it was made in 1943, the USSR was a U.S. ally. The movie was set in the USSR. Apparently, the idea that children might be happy under communism, even for a moment, might convince Americans that the system was not so bad.

Jack Warner, then president of Warner Brothers Movie Studio, made the following statement before HUAC:

Ideological termites have burrowed into many American industries, organizations, and societies. Wherever they may be, I say let us dig them out and get rid of them. My brothers and I will be happy to subscribe generously to a pest-removal fund. We are willing to establish such a fund to ship to Russia the people who don't like our American system of government and prefer the communistic system to ours. That's how strongly we feel about the subversives who want to overthrow our free American system.

If there are communists in our industry, or any other industry, organization, or society who seek to undermine our free institutions, let's find out about it and know who they are. Let the record be spread clear, for all to read and judge. The public is entitled to know the facts. And the motion-picture industry is entitled to have the public know the facts.

Our company is keenly aware of its responsibilities to keep its product free from subversive poisons. With all the vision at my command, I scrutinize the planning and production of our motion pictures. It is my firm belief that there is not a Warner Brothers picture that can fairly be judged to be hostile to our country, or communistic in tone or purpose....

McCarthy was not entirely wrong about the political beliefs held by many in Hollywood. Screenwriters, directors, and actors did tend to be liberals. Many had been members of the American Communist Party (ACP). In addition, several members of Hollywood lent their names and talent to the civil rights movement and other areas of social change. These goals were shared by the ACP. But that was not the same as wanting to violently overthrow the U.S. government

Writers targeted

More than half of those called to testify before HUAC were writers. Perhaps this was because it was the writers whose ideas were featured most directly through film. Or it may have been that they held less power and were thus easier targets than famous stars or rich executives. Whatever the case, screenwriters were the ones most likely to be "blacklisted" and cut off from their work. To be on the blacklist meant that your name was among those people that all Hollywood executives agreed not to hire.

Some writers continued to write and sell scripts under false names. Others became too upset to write. Unlike writers, actors and directors could not hide their identities. Divorce, alcoholism, and other stress-related trouble were common in the families of blacklisted people.

This is screenwriter Dalton Trumbo of the "Hollywood Ten" leaving a HUAC hearing on October 28, 1948. Trumbo shouted, "This is the beginning of American concentration camps."

Proving Loyalty

The Hollywood Ten had been the focus of HUAC attacks in 1947. In those hearings, the committee genuinely wanted to find out which of the ten were communists. The hearings held in 1951 were stranger than the 1947 hearings.

All of the witnesses called were already known by HUAC to be former members of the communist party. The idea of these hearings was to make Hollywood communists admit to their "wrongdoing" and prove they regretted their mistake by naming fellow communists. Those names were already familiar to the committee as well. A witness was not actually helping the committee so much as proving he or she had become a "loyal American."

Two-thirds of those called to testify refused to cooperate. Like the Hollywood Ten, most refused, saying that the First Amendment made the proceedings illegal. Actor Zero Mostel said that he would discuss his own actions and beliefs, but he would not name fellow communists. He said his decision was based on his religious beliefs. Mostel later portrayed a blacklisted actor in *The Front*. This 1976 film about the blacklist days was written, produced, directed, and largely acted by former blacklistees.

Other ex-communists felt there really was a dangerous communist conspiracy. They felt it was their duty as a former member to help expose it. Elia Kazan, a writer and director, was the most famous name to take the stand and reveal the names of fellow former communists. Kazan, whose films won many awards, was avoided for years by those who felt he was a traitor.

Lillian Hellman was blacklisted after refusing to cooperate with HUAC. Her play "Scoundrel Time" deals with McCarthyism and the Hollywood blacklist. In a letter to HUAC she explained that she would testify about herself, but not about others. She wrote: "I have nothing to hide from your committee and there is nothing in my life of which I am ashamed....But to hurt innocent people whom I knew many years ago in order to save myself is, to me, inhuman and indecent and dishonorable. I cannot and will not cut my conscience to fit this year's fashions..."

Kazan caused quarrels even in 1999, when he was given a lifetime achievement Academy Award. Many fellow directors, actors, and other members of the film industry refused to stand or applaud when he received the award.

Lee Grant, an actress nominated for an Academy Award, was blacklisted after she refused to testify against her first husband, screenwriter Arnold Manoff. Grant eventually returned to Hollywood and won a pair of Oscars. Most of those blacklisted were less famous and some never rebuilt their careers.

Testimony of Lionel Stander

No one's 1951 HUAC testimony was more bold than actor Lionel Stander's. Stander exasperated the committee's senators and attorneys. Stander pointed to HUAC itself as a "subversive" activity and his testimony drew laughter from some observers:

Stander: *I know of some subversion, and I can help the committee if it is really interested.*

Velde (HUAC member): *Mr. Stander–*

Stander: *I know of a group of fanatics who are desperately trying to undermine the Constitution of the United States by depriving artists and others of life, liberty and the pursuit of happiness without the process of law. If you are interested in that, I would like to tell you about it. I can tell names, I can cite instances, and I am one of the first victims of it, and if you are interested in that...*

Velde: *No, Mr Stander, let me–*

Stander: *And these people are engaged in the conspiracy, outside all the legal processes, to undermine our very fundamental American concepts upon which our entire system of jurisprudence exists–*

Velde: *Now, Mr. Stander–*

Stander: *–and who also–*

Velde: *Let me tell you this: you are a witness before this committee–*

Stander: *Well, if you are interested–*

Velde: *–a committee of the Congress of the United States–*

Stander: *–But I am willing to tell you–*

Velde: *–and you are in the same position as any other witness–*

Stander: *I am willing to tell you about these activities–*

Velde: *–regardless of your standing in the motion picture world–*

Stander: *–which I think are subversive... .*

Future President of the United States Ronald Reagan was head of the Screen Actors Guild in 1951. He regularly informed the FBI about "disloyal" actors and proudly took an anti-communist stand. Like Richard Nixon, this helped build his career in the Republican Party.

McCarthy Goes Too Far

McCarthy was reelected in 1952 and named chairman of the Senate Permanent Investigations Subcommittee (SPIS). He began launching investigations of government officials and agencies. By 1954, McCarthy had made too many enemies for his own good. An SPIS investigation of the activities of an Army dentist led to his downfall. The dentist, Major Irving Peress, had been considered "a security risk" because he had friends and associates that anti-communist forces considered questionable. He had been promoted nevertheless. McCarthy claimed that this indicated the Army was likely full of communists and he intended to find them.

The last straw

Vice-President Richard Nixon, formerly a McCarthy ally, was assigned by President Eisenhower to look for specific information to use against McCarthy. Nixon soon found that Roy Cohn, McCarthy's most trusted advisor, had provided a perfect way to attack the senator. Cohn had tried to use his influence to help a friend who had been drafted into the Army. An army base commander told of how Cohn demanded that a friend, David Schine, be allowed to skip many of his duties. When Cohn's request was denied, he went so far as to call the Secretary of the Army in the Pentagon to demand that Schine be allowed to leave the base at night.

Edward R. Murrow was one of the most respected reporters in the United States. His broadcast on March 9, 1954, drew a negative portrait of McCarthy.

McCarthy's own sub-committee decided to hold hearings on the matter. The hearings were seen and heard by a national audience on television. Near the end of the hearings, McCarthy grew desperate and made a final mistake. McCarthy told senators and the nation that a young lawyer working for the Army had been a member of the Lawyer's Guild while in law school. The Lawyer's Guild was a left-wing organization, but it was not communist. Joseph Welch, the lead attorney for the Army, had been prepared for this attack. Welch spoke slowly: "Have you no sense of decency, sir?" The nation saw that McCarthy had gone too far.

McCarthy's punishment

In December 1954, the Senate voted to censure McCarthy for "conduct contrary to senatorial tradition." This is the strongest action the Senate could take to punish a colleague other than removing him from office. It was only the third time in history such a step had been taken.

Later it was also revealed that McCarthy had accepted money from the Pepsi-Cola company in exchange for helping the company sneak around rules after World War II. Just as quickly as he had risen, McCarthy was gone. He retired from the Senate and disappeared from public life. McCarthy never apologized for any of his actions. He died of a liver condition in Bethesda, Maryland, on May 2, 1957. He was just 47 years old.

McCarthy responded to Murrow's report with an attack that made McCarthy look worse, not better.

Roy Cohn

Roy Cohn became the chief counsel (top lawyer) to the Government Committee on Operations of the Senate in 1952. He was appointed by Joseph McCarthy after J. Edgar Hoover recommended him. Cohn had helped Hoover's FBI successfully prosecute members of the American Communist Party (ACP) as well as Julius and Ethel Rosenberg.

Soon after Cohn was appointed chief counsel, he hired his best friend, David Schine, to become his consultant. After McCarthy's senate censure, Cohn was forced to resign his post. He contacted friends and managed to join a New York law firm.

Cohn made a great deal of money as a lawyer, but owed the government three million dollars in unpaid taxes. During the 1980s Cohn's luck ran out. New York State took away his license to practice law because of "unethical and unprofessional conduct." Cohn died in 1986.

Fighting McCarthy

Why didn't more people fight back against McCarthy sooner? Most people who disliked McCarthy's methods supported his intention to destroy the communist problem. Many liberals who strongly supported freedom of speech believed communists in the United States posed a threat. Even the Supreme Court failed to uphold liberty in many cases.

A few brave individuals, like actor Paul Robeson, and civil rights lawyer Abraham Fortas, repeatedly spoke out against the anti-communist witch hunts. But many of the organizations one would expect to speak against McCarthy had been weakened by years of his attacks. Others simply failed to reach agreement among its members on what to say.

ACLU

Of all the organizations in the United States, the American Civil Liberties Union (ACLU) should have complained loudly about McCarthy's tactics. The organization, formed in 1920, is dedicated to upholding freedom of speech. But the ACLU did not directly help defendants in McCarthy-era trials. It did not speak out in an effort to save the Rosenbergs from execution. A number of the ACLU's top officials were strong anti-communists who saw McCarthy's efforts as necessary to protect the country.

Other organizations failed as well. The American Bar Association (ABA), the powerful union of lawyers, did not speak out on behalf of attorneys who defended accused communists only to find their careers in danger. The American Association of University Professors failed to protest as hundreds of professors were fired for political reasons. The Screen Actors Guild, headed by Ronald Reagan, aided anti-communists in their drive to blacklist entertainment industry people labeled as reds. It was Reagan who made loyalty oaths part of getting a job in Hollywood.

Organizations that did try to speak out were spotlighted by the FBI and HUAC. Members were blacklisted and the organization was placed on a list of subversive groups. This made it difficult to attract new members and gain broader support.

The most effective way to protect oneself from an attack by McCarthy and the anti-communists was to go to court. Few people accused of subversive activity ever went to prison. Usually when the government attempted to imprison or deport known or suspected communists, the cases were delayed for long periods of time. After such delays, the cases were often thrown out of court by judges. Still, those under attack for their political beliefs often suffered worse losses—of income, reputation, and friends—than if they had served a six-month jail sentence.

A number of people took the government or employers to court to recover lost income after being blacklisted or fired. Many screenwriters and actors filed such claims. Few ever saw a penny. Such carelessly wrecked lives act as a permanent warning against crazed investigations.

McCarthyism after McCarthy

The United States that Joseph McCarthy helped create was less tolerant. McCarthyism shifted some of the country's focus during the 1960s away from communism and toward groups fighting for the civil rights of African Americans. Leaders and groups ranging from peace advocate Martin Luther King Jr. to the violent Black Panthers earned secret files in Hoover's FBI. Groups that opposed the war in Vietnam were also spied on.

The so-called "domino theory" came to rule foreign policy decisions. The theory stated that just like dominos set on their ends in a row, if one country falls to communism, the country next door will likely fall, too. Such fears led the United States to support a number of dictators and tyrants simply because they were not communists. A number of cruel governments in South and Central America, as well as in Asia, got support from the U.S. government.

During the late 1960s, the United States slowly entered the Vietnam War. Eventually, U.S. troops fought alongside South Vietnamese troops in an attempt to stop a communist takeover by North Vietnam.

Viewing McCarthy today

Some historians point out that recently released documents confirm many of McCarthy's worst fears. Known as the Venona decryptions, these decoded Soviet messages prove that there were hundreds of communist agents at work in the U.S. Further, they prove that there were members of the U.S. government working for the USSR. Some experts say the documents prove that Julius Rosenberg provided help to the USSR in building their atomic bomb. Other evidence is being used as proof that Alger Hiss was guilty of espionage.

The argument has become another one being fought by liberals and conservatives. Many members of the ACP wanted to fight social injustice in the United States for the good of all citizens. At the same time, it is clear that the ACP was being told what to do by the USSR. So, what should the U.S. government have done? That's where the argument starts.

One Chinese person alone stops tanks from advancing in Beijing in 1989. Many citizens in communist countries wanted a different system.

"McCarthy has gone down as one of the most reviled men in U.S. history, but historians are now facing the unpleasant truth that he was right," wrote a British newspaper in 1996. Another writer thought that "Point by point, McCarthy got it all wrong and yet was still closer to the truth than those who ridiculed him."

Others believe that whatever damage might have been done by Soviet spies working in the United States was nothing compared to the crimes that resulted from McCarthyism. Not only were the lives of countless innocent people damaged, but valuable ideas were never examined. No one dared discuss government-provided health care for all Americans, for example, or the value of strong labor unions, for fear of being labeled a communist. One writer argued that had the State Department not removed so many experts on China, the U.S. might have avoided getting into the Vietnam War. That anti-communist war cost the lives of more than 58,000 Americans and over one million Vietnamese.

Timeline

1895	J. Edgar Hoover is born in Washington, D.C.
1909	Joseph McCarthy is born in Grand Chute, Wisconsin
1917	Hoover takes a job with the U.S. Department of Justice
1919	The American Communist Party (ACP) is founded
	Hoover is put in charge of the "Palmer Raids"
1924	Hoover takes over what will soon become the FBI
1938	Congress forms the House Un-American Activities Committee (HUAC)
1939	Whittaker Chambers testifies before HUAC and confesses that he spied for the USSR. He also testifies that Alger Hiss gave him secret State Department documents.
1940	The Smith Act passes, making it illegal for anyone to argue in favor of, or make any sort of plans for, the overthrow of the U.S. government by force
1944	Joseph McCarthy loses election to the U.S. Senate
1945	Germany surrenders to Allied forces and World War II ends
1946	Joseph McCarthy wins election to the U.S. Senate
1947	HUAC looks into communist influence in movies and names the Hollywood Ten
	Hoover testifies before HUAC about the dangers posed to U.S. by subversives
	President Truman signs Executive Order 9835, increasing the power of the FBI
	Movie studios announce that the Hollywood Ten in their employ would be fired—it becomes known as "the blacklist"
1948	The Hollywood Ten are found guilty of contempt of Congress and serve six-month prison terms
	A hollowed-out pumpkin containing microfilm is found on Whittaker Chambers's farm in Maryland. The microfilm, containing State Department documents, was supposedly given to Chambers by Alger Hiss. The film becomes known as the "pumpkin papers."
1949	China becomes a communist nation
	The National Education Association and the American Association of School Administrators sends booklets to teachers on guidelines for teaching "Americanism"
	The University of California at Berkeley requires professors to sign an oath of loyalty to the United States. Many professors refuse or protest.
	Truman announces that the USSR has exploded its own atomic bomb
1950	McCarthy makes a famous speech in Wheeling, West Virginia, in which he claims that several employees of the U.S. State Department are communists